IT'S TIME TO EAT VEGAN CARROT SOUP

It's Time to Eat VEGAN CARROT SOUP

Walter the Educator

Silent King Books
A WhichHead Entertainment Imprint

Copyright © 2024 by Walter the Educator

All rights reserved. No part of this book may be reproduced in any manner whatsoever without written per- mission except in the case of brief quotations embodied in critical articles and reviews.

First Printing, 2024

Disclaimer

This book is a literary work; the story is not about specific persons, locations, situations, and/or circumstances unless mentioned in a historical context. Any resemblance to real persons, locations, situations, and/or circumstances is coincidental. This book is for entertainment and informational purposes only. The author and publisher offer this information without warranties expressed or implied. No matter the grounds, neither the author nor the publisher will be accountable for any losses, injuries, or other damages caused by the reader's use of this book. The use of this book acknowledges an understanding and acceptance of this disclaimer.

It's Time to Eat VEGAN CARROT SOUP is a collectible early learning book by Walter the Educator suitable for all ages belonging to Walter the Educator's Time to Eat Book Series. Collect more books at WaltertheEducator.com

USE THE EXTRA SPACE TO TAKE NOTES AND DOCUMENT YOUR MEMORIES

VEGAN CARROT SOUP

It's time to eat, hooray, hooray!

It's Time to Eat Vegan Carrot Soup

The soup is ready, we've waited all day.

Bright orange carrots in a steamy bowl,

A tasty treat to warm your soul.

The carrots cook, soft and sweet,

Blended up, they're fun to eat!

A swirl of spice, a pinch of love,

It's like sunshine in a mug.

We add coconut milk, creamy and light,

To make it smooth and oh-so-bright.

With every sip, it's pure delight,

A hug in a bowl on a chilly night.

Sprinkle some parsley on the top,

Or crunchy seeds for a little pop!

Dip some bread, it's oh so yummy,

Vegan carrot soup fills your tummy.

It's Time to Eat

Vegan Carrot Soup

Packed with goodness, it's healthy too,

For eyes, for skin, and for me and you!

Carrots bring the power, strong and sweet,

A veggie so special, they can't be beat.

Share with your family, share with a friend,

This kind of soup is a joy to lend.

Made with love and gentle care,

Vegan carrot soup is meant to share.

It's so simple, it's so fun,

Making soup for everyone.

Stirring the pot, the bubbles rise,

The scent of carrots is a sweet surprise.

Eating plants is kind and cool,

Good for the earth and a helpful rule.

With every spoonful, feel the cheer,

It's Time to Eat Vegan Carrot Soup

Carrot soup smiles from ear to ear.

So grab your bowl, your spoon, your seat,

The soup is warm and ready to eat!

Take a big bite, it's silky and sweet,

Vegan carrot soup is the ultimate treat.

When the soup is gone, don't feel blue,

We'll make more carrots just for you!

Cooking together is a lovely thing,

It's Time to Eat

Vegan Carrot Soup

With carrot soup, we'll dance and sing!

ABOUT THE CREATOR

Walter the Educator is one of the pseudonyms for Walter Anderson. Formally educated in Chemistry, Business, and Education, he is an educator, an author, a diverse entrepreneur, and he is the son of a disabled war veteran. "Walter the Educator" shares his time between educating and creating. He holds interests and owns several creative projects that entertain, enlighten, enhance, and educate, hoping to inspire and motivate you. Follow, find new works, and stay up to date with Walter the Educator™

at WaltertheEducator.com

www.ingramcontent.com/pod-product-compliance
Lightning Source LLC
LaVergne TN
LVHW052016060526
838201LV00059B/4049